THE
DEATH
METAL
PASTORALS

THE
DEATH
METAL
PASTORALS

POEMS

RYAN PATRICK SMITH

Black
Lawrence
Press

www.blacklawrence.com

Executive Editor: Diane Goettel
Chapbook Editor: Kit Frick
Book and Cover Design: Amy Freels
Cover Art: "busts" (2013, graphite & gouache) by Connie Mae Oliver.
Used with permission.

Published 2019 by Black Lawrence Press.
Printed in the United States.

CONTENTS

Augury   I

Escape from Milam Landfill   2

Construction: Georgetown, Ky.   3

At the beginning of the concert, the singer explains that she is
on her way to Boulder to watch her mother die   5

Deathmetalpastoral   6

OF BEING TRANSMITTED ON A SILVERY ALIEN WHEEL   7

Deathmetalpastoral   8

Deathmetalpastoral   9

Sarah Connor Chronicles Apocalypse   10

As Mister Rogers Prays to His Aquarium   11

What A Weird Tenor This World Is, How It Lends The
Appearance Of Appearing Like Something Else   12

Deathmetalpastoral   13

Playing the Icon   14

Raccoons Possums Strays   15

Deathmetalpastoral   16

Pantoum Before The Law   17

The Gods Mortals The Earth Shoes The Temple The Sky The Bridge
The Jug The Fourfold The Poem Pain The Threshold
The Difference & Stillness   21

Deathmetalpastoral   23

Acknowledgments   25

Notes   27

Augury

Reader in your dark red car. The starlings hear the dwindle.
They hear the nozzles of a service station's blue pumps rasp,

the grease trucks filling up behind a neighboring diner, see
every sign raised high on its pole. Read them this way.

They sing to one another in the tree that overhangs the
world's flat roofs, adjust

their feathers like a bevy of hatchets.

Read them this way. The starlings smell famine nearby &
trouble coming the way someone tracking through woods smells rot
in the dark

& know there is a time to eat and time for exile, that nothing
works here but blood & radio. Murmuration. They unfurl against a
low sky into an open script. & know it is time for you, the sky in dusk
& sign-starred,

wondrous. Get out, lock your doors. Get scissors & net, climb
a ladder & haul starlings from the wind. Split their caustic chests.
Track where the steam drifts in the light.

Escape from Milam Landfill

. . . the premier celebrity resident of Arcadia is Death.
—Joyelle McSweeney, *The Necropastoral: Poetry, Media, Occults*

What's manna, what's milk. What's demonic to a mountain,
the Illinois trash-mound chronic

with sourness & leak. Nothing fell on you like preserving
snow, or petrified your leftovers. No container evaded breaking. In
the oily emulsion of stars, only the spoiled cream of chicken, the
chrome of lost teeth. Do not remove your

plasma from the screen. In something slightly less than this,
suspend yourself. As a spurting floats its arc, mark it, the place where
you are, with a blown-out eye. That boy who killed his father, remem-
ber him. Hunting. Mistaken squirrel-shot, & his father fell. The fun-
dament did not erode. But something went away. Gleaner, forager,

a year from then, the singular celebrity of your life: she dies,
too. & the hours of the day it happened begin to behave in a certain
way. Self-organize. Emerge, entranced by the beauty of their own
splatter in a craze of glass. Relax, lover of echo, reflection: you are
only a pattern. Reflection, lover of echo. Spent & dried like glue. You
are only holding a balloon. & it is tethered by a string. & it is an eye-
ball chained to the skull.

& how the chain would snap. & what severs filament from
bulb. There is no connotation, only meat/no breeze, only seed. How
will the balloon go anywhere. When you let it go. Where will it go. It
rises to the sky of dead, you were told, a messenger of less than air.

Construction: Georgetown, Ky.

Adrift in the sun, I walk the roadside edge of the vast

field. The hours of the summer above me,

pack-like, as though they have slept here.

The frame of the one house up now

half-dressed, the tarp draped loose as my own mother's knot

of hair in the morning.

And it's how the sky raises the sun

above its head, then has to bury it,

over and over, that I remember things,

how the farmland here, once excavated, reveals

the neighborhood it will soon become,

that I recall the handful of oilbright wood rosary

in a velvet bag, each bead a mother or father

saying *we will soon be lost*, each one a prayer to answer to.

They will dig a pit for the swimming

pool, warm, aglow at night with sunken lights

and the gathering mysteries

of small stones, the ghost boats of beetle husks.

Now, they call from the middle of their rafts.

At the hour of our death. Say something back,

and leave them in the water.

At the beginning of the concert, the singer explains that she is on her way to Boulder to watch her mother die

Then what is the maraschino cherry in Jason's Manhattan,
bathed by the liquor's ice-water honey. What is she doing here

singing, what is it to her, to me, to be

with her. What is it to her or me, is it like the back porch last
week budded with ladybugs hungry to winter. The ceiling's & the
posts' & the railings' stain of black-flecked redness, the spraying of
pheromones, if thickening is another way to gather

fortune. Everything dies on a wave. If at the peak rides super-
fluous sugar, the wave's valley flowering with clapping, as the lyric's
last note tapers to low hills, goldenrod. If this is the applause,

this is the applause, the syrup thick, blood-thick preserva-
tive. The singer blood, singing blood singing another song in which
the mother is bathing like a single, unspoiled fruit.

Deathmetalpastoral

the swain who is on the cusp of somewhere

Furrows once rowed with tall stalks of tobacco, my bone marrow, the scarecrow-absent

field. Black barn full of wooden stakes & straw, smell of ghost-smoke from a twenty-years-ago harvesting. *Burning crop of disease.* On the other side of the stone wall border, burn pile piled high with the viscera of uselessness, the ribbing, the limbs, the old upholstery. My burn-pile's employer

the master of the field; you can see him in summer by the garden fired up with sun. I am twigs of angel's trumpet, fallen; when I was a boy I wore the flowers of the tree on my fingers, wore them as claws, a monster of petals. My life's with my ex

my ex is a sweetgum, shells and star-leaves scattered on the lawn. *I am just a spectator, an advocate*

documenting the loss. I yank out all the weeds, I gather them up. Then I am in a pickup headed for the branches threshed by the thunderstorm, wheels churning to the blast-beat death-drums in the tape deck. I want to burn the trees, & I want to burn the enemies. *Infecting the roots in an instant.*

Where am I, where am I in the field that I give my will over to you?

OF BEING TRANSMITTED ON A SILVERY ALIEN WHEEL

Last night's songbird. Tonight's theremin or kite. Owls, abduction. Alighting lights. We each had dreamed a calling, a cantillating dove, transmission, telepathy, elation. Were or were not of the same mind or neither, the same kind or hybrid. In a sedan on fire or not on fire, or the cottage on the waste of a highway's long strip. Then lab or labyrinth. Pristine bone or carving on a plinth of crystal, cool master

breath. This is how and why we break and share our bodies, divide and share our black eyes and our blood, inviting. They did sleep with us. Their lights strobed. Widening forceps, stirrups, cortex, lobe. Predicate or delicate nurses, load us

into syntax, section by section. Sentence, helix. Of legs and hips, naked backs that thrum with rays, light rain or whatever it is. Of ribs. Transformative coding. The codeine-slow crawl of each emission. Transitional visions, each passed like a glass and pressed with palm-prints. The logbooks of your clinics, pressed with gray erasures. We are now nothing more

than cases, tooth-shaped, blurred with abscess. Tender, wonderful, painful brain-pans, egg-space, hollowed pillar. Our white skies clear, bereft of messages. We passengers.

Deathmetalpastoral

the swain who is swooning for a wood full of birds

        Dear Body of My Other—you are metal as the ring of the tuning fork & down-tuned v-body of your insomnia, as pig-iron blown for nails, screws & cutlery. You are the wetness of a fist of baby,

        the winter crust of your sweat, the top of your left tit over your breastbone, your armpits, the seven birds tattooed on your neck & the vulture of your shoulder, the bare dips behind your knees covered with buzzard waste, the rivulets molting from the black wire of your labia to your anus, fit & strapping

        like young men are strapping & you are lit

        like the blood of your irises, the death-growl

        of your breathing hard & sick. Please

        hold me down in the field in the metal-brown bark of your trees & your licking hurts.

Deathmetalpastoral

the swain who is exhausted from all harvesting

High gold, holy noon: eradicate the shadows, ignite the wool.
I lay down a long leg and elegant toe and let you

buckle my sandal, eyes on the horizon, helicopter of vultures.
I puff an honest cough from my chest. My hard skin is a flute.

When nature's necklace was clipped, the pearls sprayed
everywhere on the cowering soil. When the tractors placed their
tracks,

green life scraped from copper vaults. I gave my avatar a kiss.
I hang the chandelier of bones.

Sarah Connor Chronicles Apocalypse

This is the physics Sarah Connor teaches in her dream. In episode three, Los Alamos physicists iced against a constellated blackboard, she demonstrates the inertia of gunfire, she & prophecy

wrestling like heroic scorpions. Dear John, dear endoskeletal stamina & the judgment of machines, she says in messages to the future resistance: we are the same titanium beneath our different disguises. Dear Terminator and Los Angeles: when I was 19, & my hair feathered down my shoulders, you came for me,

anointed me in an everlasting diner light. Dear Kyle Reese, I came with you when you told me if I came, then I would live. You made me pop and glisten like a frying fish; we made each other

a room, piped it full of smoke & music. We've been multiplying timelines, child after child after

child sent to kill me, & I will never die. I mother my body like a wolf. I am your judge now, Los Angeles past present and future, & I rend my judgment like the cloth of grief. Send me your brother, & I will make him grieve, send me a daughter to protect me & I will make her grieve. & we are watching the season pass

on television, my love and I, water spinning through myriad bones, a cricket singing in our northern wall. I trace the veer of her hair to the scalp. I crush my face against her spine.

As Mister Rogers Prays to His Aquarium

as the kingdom we imagine has a train, and the train has a
station in our house. as the glass spun gold with you who swim your
lives together,

as the gold of our life to come. as every new flake draws
another mouth to the surface of the water. as each ripple is not sound,
but hunger. as the difference between silence and the word

after. as these are our words: circle, stillness. spiral, pause.
every new day is a machine of transformation,

even the newest dead, as though the water held us moving by
the wire of. as one drawn to another by the wire of. another whorl in
the spiral. another arm. a new line drawn in the palm.

What A Weird Tenor This World Is, How It Lends The Appearance Of Appearing Like Something Else

after a line by Kerri Webster

The little kid drives a toy cab whose body is a grocery cart that his father is pushing. The little kids next door sashay through the tank of an above-ground pool. Every little kid is learning to have a singing voice, to lose it. Various collisions like dishes being washed,

the splash of toy brass. Boy soprano. When you came home from San Juan, you said you had a dream of our bodies combined in a little girl. This was just momentary. The little kid's blinded cry in the Marco

Polo game. For the rest of her life she will shut her eyes and call out the same name, confusing the answer with the touch of a place where she can go no further. This is all just a catalogue of appearances

and most will be. Before the last word, a question asked by a passing man. Light obsessively polishes the two rare nickels of his irises. Our faces are shy in different ways. The last word is *forgotten*.

Deathmetalpastoral

the swain who is lost

First words spoken in the woods, among birches, among
downed trees the bark dulled silver of an unlooped necklace / first
words *we* first *hem* or *secrecy*, or what brambles might proffer or the
chicken wire fencing sectioning our wood from the other /

    forest & thorn, the tale played out with crows the distant
words on the vellum of understory /

    the way of glass, the way of weeds. You can pick the pathway.
You can take the pins & pinch their heads, tell me how small a longing
is & how it fits /

    in your forefinger and thumb. I will go with you / still. & if
the trees' limbs above us crosshatch into a nightness, then the leaves
are fog around the stars. Or are smoke. Or what describing would
never tell us: that the far-off utterances are trucks, maybe crashing,
maybe horses /

    voice on voice like two shattering bottles. What collision is,
our shins against the tall red growths of this wood where suns want
invitation, want clearing, these horses we will never let in.

Playing the Icon

The icon on cable sets his music on fire under the stiff black wing of his grand piano. He hammers

the keys like meat, prods them with his sticks, they start & fall apart like ash or shadow, the white & black of heat. When all the audience hears the

keyboard startle, sees the blue insistence of his fire, they are blown like seedling silk, & you are risen from the carpeted floor's lint-froth and blue burrs,

making & unmaking your hands, your teeth. Afterward, you go outside &

gather up the blades of maple pods in two fistfuls of dry molt. You fling them ahead of you,

run as they chopper back to the scuffs of gray-white gravel, as though you are the swiftest of all seeds.

Raccoons Possums Strays

living on the hill delivered us / when the creek flooded. We
were captive / kept from school our parents from work, waking up
marooned

to find the land a whale / a mammal vastness. it was always an
animal, & we lived on its back / rising & eating / wandering

& digging tiny grave-holes for the dead animals who'd fouled
a recess in the cellar or springtime sloughs of grass.

& no one could know the number of raccoons, possums,
strays / for whom the flooding of the creek was catastrophe / the banks
overrun / the killing road that twisted like a gut & my mother wrote

the city, erect a warning, stop the crosses flourishing road-
side like vine-

stems sucking on another day. this road made wide & straight
at last / thick & bitter creek. it was a made thing that we woke to. it was
made silent / void of thunder, that we slept through the rain's hard
working, the driving of its nails.

Deathmetalpastoral

the disturbed swain

Black is the color of arrowheads.

The electrical color of the wire that sways in the weight of birds' wings over the dirt

where we dug up the arrowheads. The color of the dirt and the limestone like a breastbone.

The brain of our cancerous dog was bulleted clean. The color of his deadness.

The color of the grave-loam on the land's oldest edge where a little girl is buried under.

The color of the date and the year that I slipped on once on the rain-wet rock,

eight years old, and purple is the color of the welt of the plum.

The cows of our neighbor groan from the woods. The arrows of summer will lead to water.

The apples have fallen like pin-drops of blood on the dry grass and vanished.

There is a whetstone sinking under its own weight and age, big as an altar, and you will see it if you just keep running home.

Pantoum Before The Law

For Alexis Templeton and Brittany Ferrell, arrested August 10, 2015

Before the law, says the title. Before the law, the title says:
Before the Law stands a doorkeeper.
It is therefore not as narrative that we define
the law of the name or the name of the law.

//

Before the law is a doorkeeper. A. punched the motherfucker
through the open window, the charges say, the law of the name and
the name of the law, but take note: I am powerful. And I am only the
least of the doorkeepers.

//

A. punched the motherfucker through the open window. B.
kicked the SUV, the charges say, as it plowed through A. and B.,
through all. But take note: I am powerful, and I am only the least of
the doorkeepers. Their purpose, to delay the rush hour, the daily
white flight.

//

B. kicked the motherfucker's vehicle, the charges say, causing
$5,000 worth of damages. *There's nothing there*, I said in a barely trans-
latable way. This implied: it must be questioned. The purpose of the
protest, said to delay the flight—isn't this what the doorkeeper says?
Isn't it "there is a place for you here"—there is a place for you? For
what, we don't know, but there is a place,

it was barely translated. It must be questioned, that during these many years A. and B. forget the other doorkeepers, and this first one seems the sole obstacle preventing access to the Law. There is a place for them, they don't know for what, but there is a place. This literature itself makes law, emerging in the place where law is made.

//

During these years they still remember the other doorkeepers. B. said, *My two days spent in jail have made me stronger.* This literature itself makes law, emerging in the place where law is made, charged with assault, trespassing, peace disturbance, released early Wednesday afternoon.

//

My two days spent in jail have made me stronger, said B., and *I,* the narrative "I" can scare the Law shitless, *have ventured glosses, multiplied interpretations, asked and diverted questions, left enigmas intact, accused, defended, praised, subpoenaed, charged with assault, trespassing, peace disturbance, been freed after posting ten percent of a $10,000 bail. It's beautiful,* she said.

//

Accused, acquitted, defended, praised, subpoenaed: under these conditions literature can play the law, trespass and disturb the peace, then free it after posting bail. It's beautiful: we find there the same content with different boundaries and above all without a proper title,

and under these conditions she can play the law, a region whose frontiers would be pure and its titles indivisible—unbruised body, unblackened eyes. Since the gate stands open as usual, A. and

B. stoop to peer through the gateway. They find there the same content with a different set of boundaries, aware of the shit that exhausts from the gateway of the Law.

//

Since the gate stands open as usual, they step to one side. They'd found out the origin of the law and had a nose for this kind of thing, aware of the shit that steams from the gateway of the Law. The characters in the story, the doorkeeper and A. and B., are all before the law, but one of them turns their back on the law and yet pulls up before it.

//

They'd found out the origins of the law and had a nose for this particular shit. The protagonists are all before the law but in opposition, on either side of a line of inversion. The spray of exhaust from the pipe and the entitling sequence describe the one who turns her back on the law, in order to prohibit all presentation—the women who face the law see no more than its back, for the law is prohibition and prohibited. Noun and attribute.

//

A. gave the motherfucker in the vehicle a black eye—the black eye is the charge on either side of the line. Invert the black eye, the charge, and the line, and behind them stands no one. For the law is prohibition and prohibited. Noun and attribute. A. and B., since they are before the law, since they cannot enter it, they are also outside the law, they are outlaws.

//

And behind them stands no one, the chain is broken. The law guards itself, a doorkeeper who guards nothing, the door remaining open on nothing. But because A. and B. are before the law, because they cannot enter it, thrashing at metal, lashing through a window of air. They are outlaws. Because the driver is inside the vehicle they are not outlaw they are somewhere where we are, the Law itself driving away.

//

The Law then would not stand up—in fact, the whole scenography of the story would be a drama of standing and sitting

a drama of nothing only the drama.

It is therefore not as narrative that we define

the doorkeeper who recognizes they have reached their end, and to let their failing senses catch the words, roars in their ears, *No one else could ever be admitted, since this gate was made only for you. I am now going to shut it.*

The Gods Mortals The Earth Shoes The Temple The Sky The Bridge The Jug The Fourfold The Poem Pain The Threshold The Difference & Stillness

For Ferguson, Mo. & Michael Brown

QuikTrip of gas-slicks of broken-down rainbowed light

burned out & had to be ruined & had to be stripped down.
Now little fires are all around, passing hand to hand: graffiti-stained-
glass, frescoed pumps,

flames on the ends of wicks vigil & remembering.

One girl, undercover in her camo head, a bandanna pouring
its red mask over her mouth, sheer

Thursday night's surveilled stomach dark below the knotted

Che of her T-shirt, sneakers packing slender, dangerous feet,
throws in her share of tonight's

leonine poses, fists' rites, quotes NWA in stereo-black on her
cardboard, like she knows the ones

who send their bright white dove to touch her like she is the
newly baptized: fuck them. Everyone who led her, singing, straight
through day into tonight's garden,

bridge-crossing. Fuck them, fuck them. Closes her fist around a candle's neck until the wax in her fingers is running like milk,

until the milk in her jug is running over her eyes like the word *flame*

runs over *fire*, the word *gas* over *tear*. Somebody already asking,

who's That Masked Black Girl, thinking it's a question. & she looks into the camera & closes her fist into stillness.

Deathmetalpastoral

the last swain

The stockyards are burning. The news breaks black-lunged, choir, radar.

In jeans of robin's egg I dressed myself today. In grass-rub & honey-dirt doe-freckling my dream calves.

I woke up on a sofa in the garage of my employer's land. I fanned my palms across my loamy beard.

Before I woke I could see myself coming like sunrise, before I turned

to TV & the yards were burning & I saw

the whirlwind, network of blackbirds & buzzards / ravenous hawks.

Now my hair now hide now nipples now loin now stomach & the many organs

now heart & lungs now blood & milk

are all burned away

into the charred black tire rolling the screen & sky.

Ruminant beauty, thinking flame,

Keep going.

Into flight.

Into the meat of you I love.

ACKNOWLEDGMENTS

Thank you to the editors of the following journals, where versions of these poems first appeared:

Kenyon Review: "Augury" and "Escape from Milam Landfill"

Salt Hill: "Construction: Georgetown, Ky."

Boston Review: "OF BEING TRANSMITTED ON A SILVERY ALIEN WHEEL"

Jet Fuel Review: "At the beginning of the concert, the singer explains that she is on her way to Boulder to watch her mother die," "What A Weird Tenor This World Is, How It Lends The Appearance of Appearing Like Something Else," and "Playing the Icon"

Burnside Review: "Deathmetalpastoral [the disturbed swain]" and "Deathmetalpastoral [the swain who is lost]"

Birdfeast: "As Mister Rogers Prays to His Aquarium"

FEELINGS: "Deathmetalpastoral [the swain who is on the cusp of somewhere]," "Deathmetalpastoral [the swain who is exhausted from all harvesting]," and "Sarah Connor Chronicles Apocalypse"

DIAGRAM: "The Gods Mortals The Earth Shoes The Temple The Sky The Bridge The Jug The Fourfold The Poem Pain The Threshold The Difference & Stillness"

Thank you also to the following early readers of these poems and this chapbook, for all of their advice and support: Shane Seely & Jennifer Tappenden.

Most of all, thank you to Brigitte Leschhorn—the first and last reader of everything.

NOTES

"Deathmetalpastoral [the swain who is on the cusp of somewhere]":
Italicized phrases are taken from the song "Blackwater Park" (2001)
by Opeth. Lyric transcriptions are from darklyrics.com.

"Deathmetalpastoral [the swain who is exhausted from all
harvesting]": This poem is a cento comprised of lyrics from the songs
"High Gold," "Glory Bronze," Red Crown," "Harmonia,"
"Returner," "True Will," and "Sun of Light" by Liturgy, from the
album *Aesthethica* (2011). Lyric transcriptions are from darklyrics.com.

"The Gods Mortals The Earth Shoes The Temple The Sky The Bridge
The Jug The Fourfold The Poem Pain The Threshold, The Difference
& Stillness": The title is taken from the translator's introduction to
Martin Heidegger's *Poetry, Language, Thought*.

"Pantoum Before The Law": This "pantoum," to call it such, is made
of quotations from Jacques Derrida's essay "Before the Law" on Franz
Kafka's parable of the same name; from Kafka's "Before the Law,"
reprinted in an English translation at the beginning of Derrida's
essay; and from the *St. Louis Post-Dispatch* article "2 Ferguson activists
charged with attacking driver during I-70 shutdown" on the arrest of
two activist leaders, Alexis Templeton and Brittany Ferrell, in
connection with a highway blockage organized for the anniversary of
Michael Brown's shooting by a Ferguson police officer. Templeton
and Ferrell met in August 2014 while taking part in the
demonstrations that followed the shooting of Brown. After
co-founding Millennial Activists United, they married in December
2014. Quotations from all sources have been freely modified, with the
exception of direct quotations of Ferrell and Templeton.

"What A Weird Tenor This World Is, How It Lends The Appearance Of Appearing Like Something Else": The title is taken from a sentence in Kerri Webster's prose poem sequence "Atomic Clock."

Ryan Patrick Smith is a poet whose work has previously appeared in the *Kenyon Review*, *Boston Review*, *DIAGRAM*, and elsewhere. He is an associate editor for *Boulevard Magazine* and teaches in the MFA in Writing program of Lindenwood University. A Kentucky native, he has lived in Lexington, Kentucky and St. Louis, Missouri; right now, he resides with his spouse in Connecticut. *The Death Metal Pastorals* is his debut chapbook.